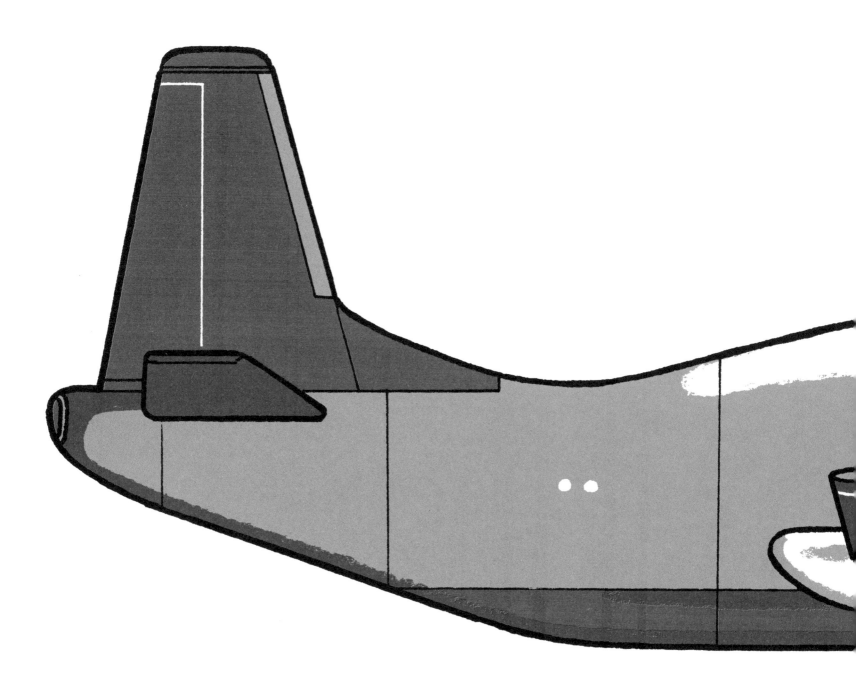

HOW BIG IS BIG?
HOW FAR IS FAR?

Illustrated by Jan Van Der Veken

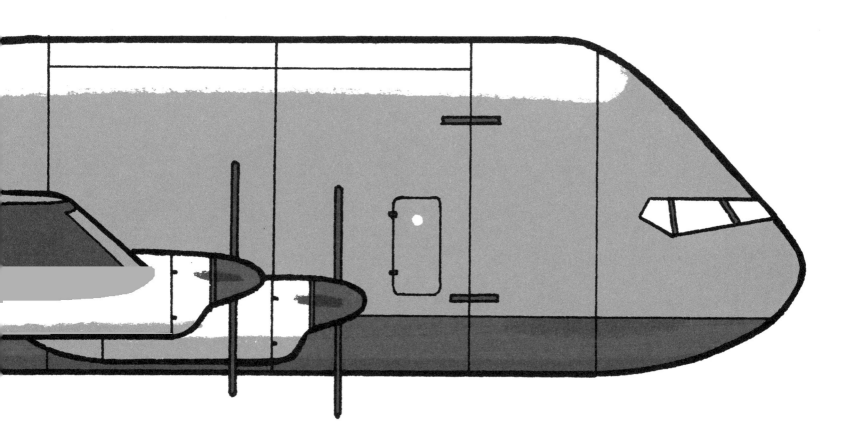

LITTLE
Gestalten

HOW BIG?

Depending on who or what you are standing next to, you can feel either very short or very tall. Next to you a cat seems very small, yet it looks like a giant to the eyes of an insect. Similarly, we might think giraffes are intimidatingly tall, yet dinosaurs would be unimpressed as they are barely their height.

0.01 inches   **20 inches**   **5.5 feet**   **16 feet**

20 feet

HOW BIG?

The Earth used to be home to animals that were much bigger than the ones that are alive today. Just think of the dinosaurs. Scientists in Argentina recently dug up giant dinosaur bones, and one of the thighbones was taller than a full-grown man!

5.9 feet   6.6 feet

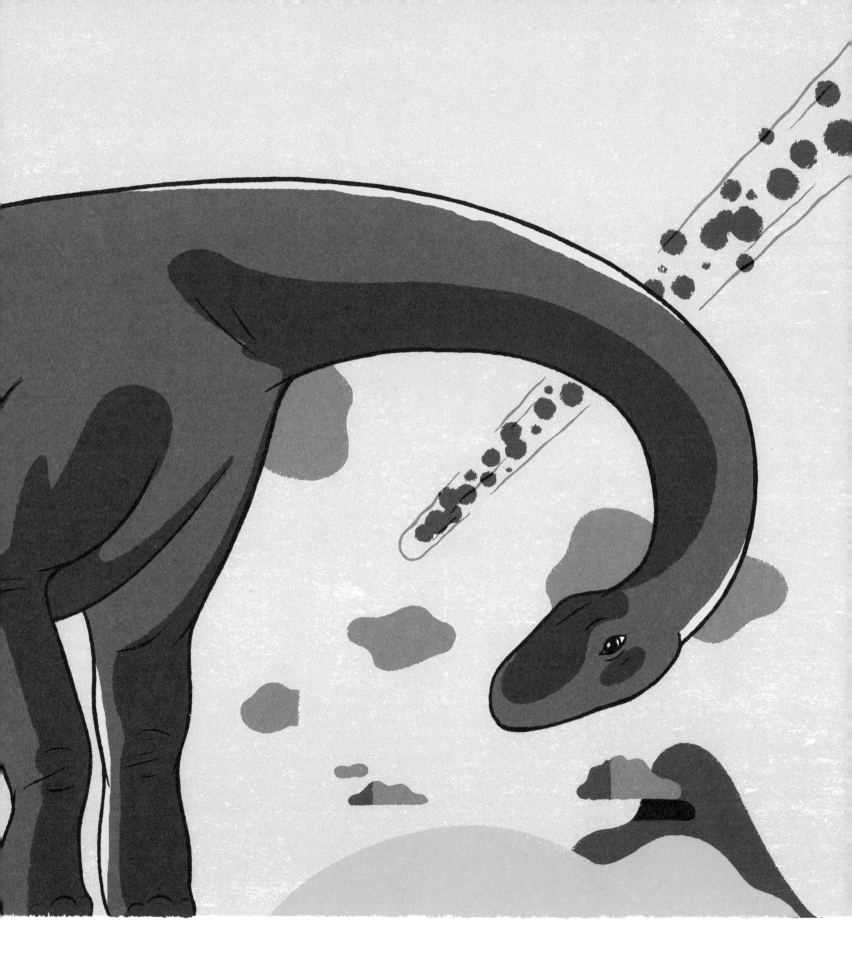

HOW HEAVY?

Clouds are made of water hanging in the air. Although they look as light as marshmallows, they're actually unbelievably heavy. A typical fair-weather cloud that you see on a summer day weighs between 11,000 and 22,000 pounds. If you were to wring it out and collect all the water, you'd end up with 1,250 to 2,500 gallons of the stuff. That's enough to fill (depending on the size) 36 to 72 bathtubs or 500 to 1,000 water buckets!

2.5 gallons   **50 gallons**

1,250 to 2,500 gallons

HOW HEAVY?

The dark clouds that gather before a summer storm are even heavier. They can hold more than 1.5 million tons of water on average. You could use that to fill more than 7.5 million bathtubs or fill 1,600 swimming pools that are 82 feet long, 41 feet wide and 3 meters deep. Here are some other things that weigh about 1.5 million tons: 150,000 school buses, 7,500 long freight trains, and 15 aircraft carriers.

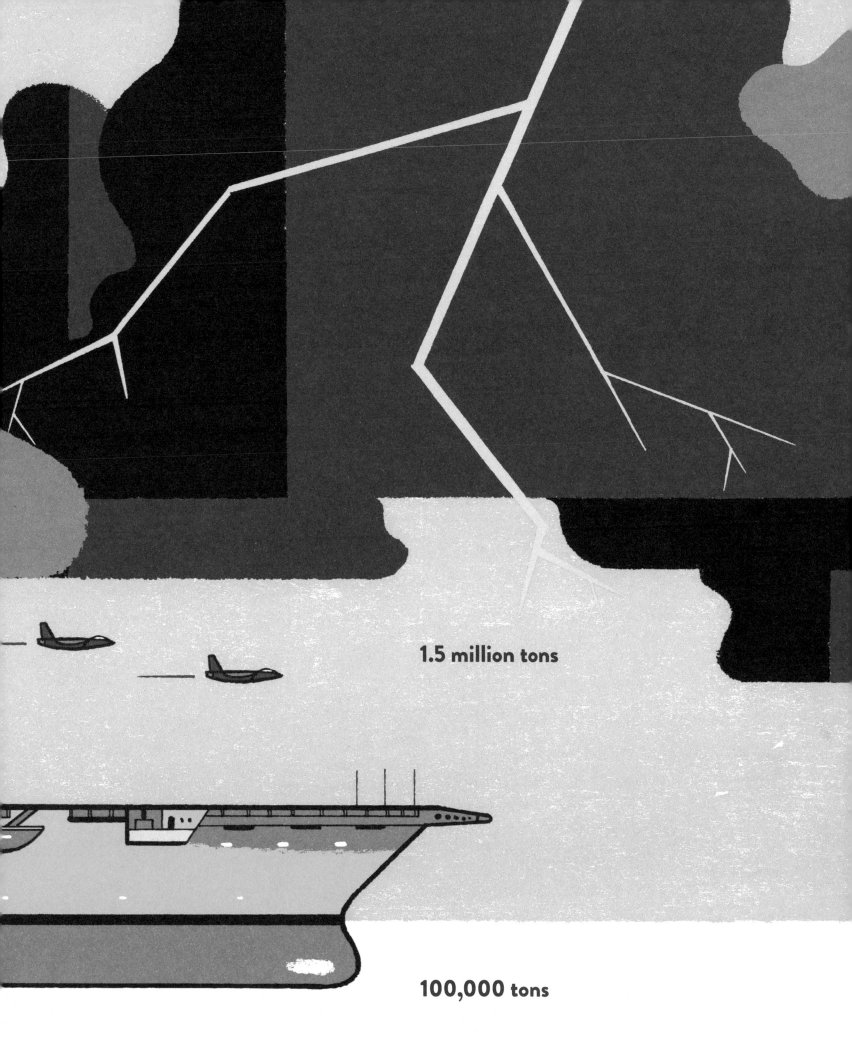

1.5 million tons

100,000 tons

HOW HEAVY?

The size of an object often tells you very little about its weight.
The Queen of England's crown, for instance, is hardly enormous,
but it weighs 75 servings of cotton candy.
Imagine what she'd look like with all that spun sugar on her head!

1 ounce

75 ounces

HOW FAST?

It takes ages to travel around the world. If you went on foot, walked at about 2.5 miles per hour and never took a break, you'd be home in one year, seven weeks, and three days. If you went by car and drove nonstop at 75 miles per hour, you'd be home in about two weeks. If you flew in a passenger plane at approximately 560 miles per hour, you'd be home in two days.

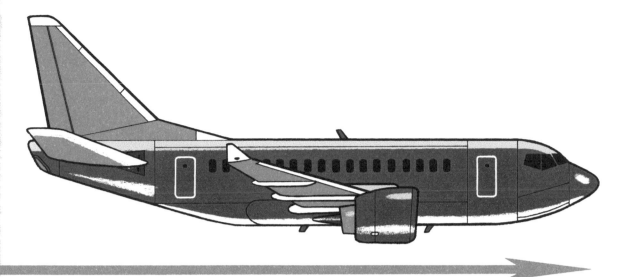

2 days

14 days

417 days

HOW FAST?

But it would take much, much longer to travel around the sun. If you went by car and drove at 75 miles per hour, you'd be on the road for about four years. If you flew in a passenger plane at about 560 miles per hour, you'd be in the air for roughly seven months.

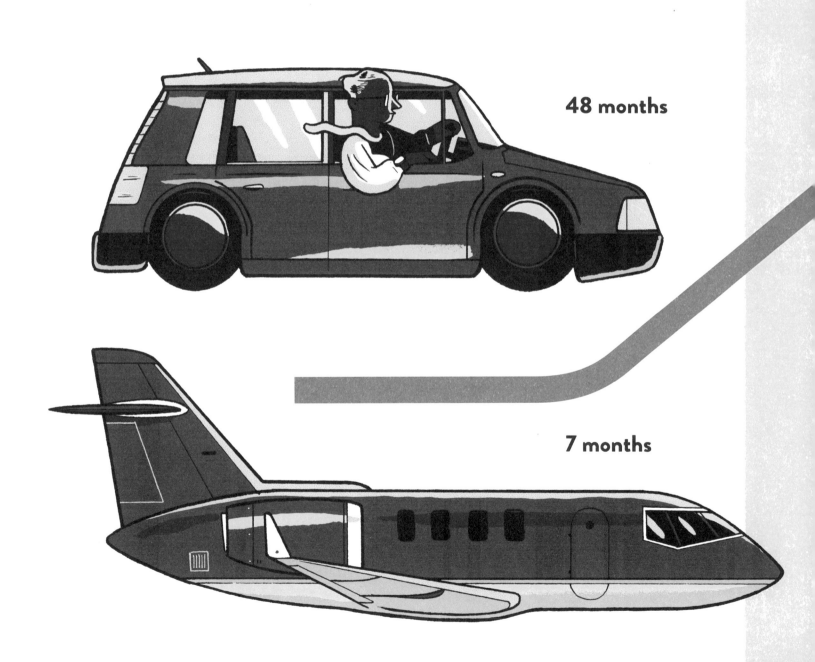

48 months

7 months

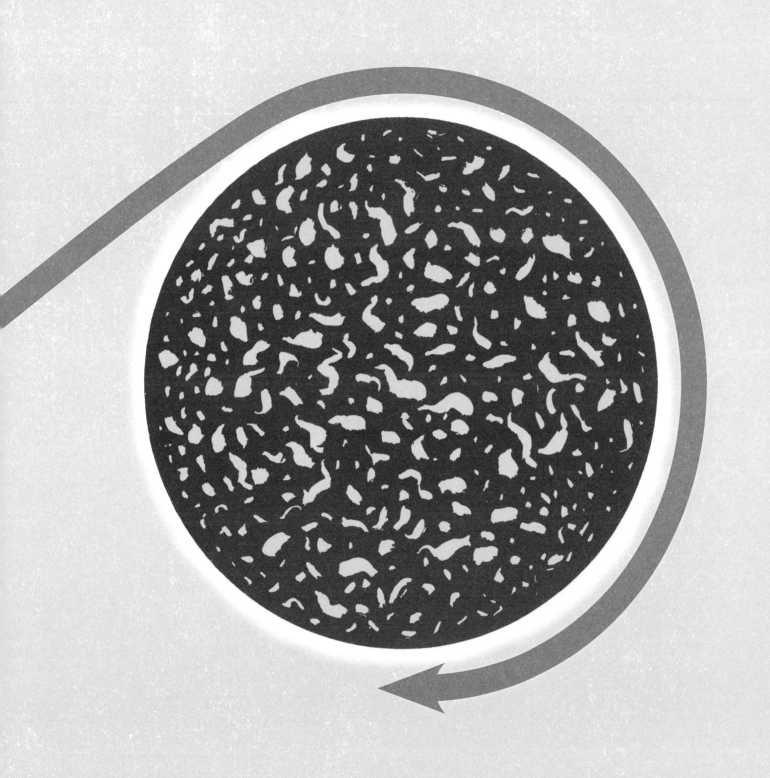

HOW FAR?

It's more or less impossible to picture how big space is. Take the sun, for example: it is so huge that if it were a ball three feet in diameter, then Earth would be the size of a cherry and Mars would be a pea.

The sun and the Earth are also really, really far apart. How far? Well, if we pretended that space was a soccer pitch and put the ball (the sun) next to one set of goalposts, then the cherry (Earth) would be sitting all the way at the opposite end of the field.

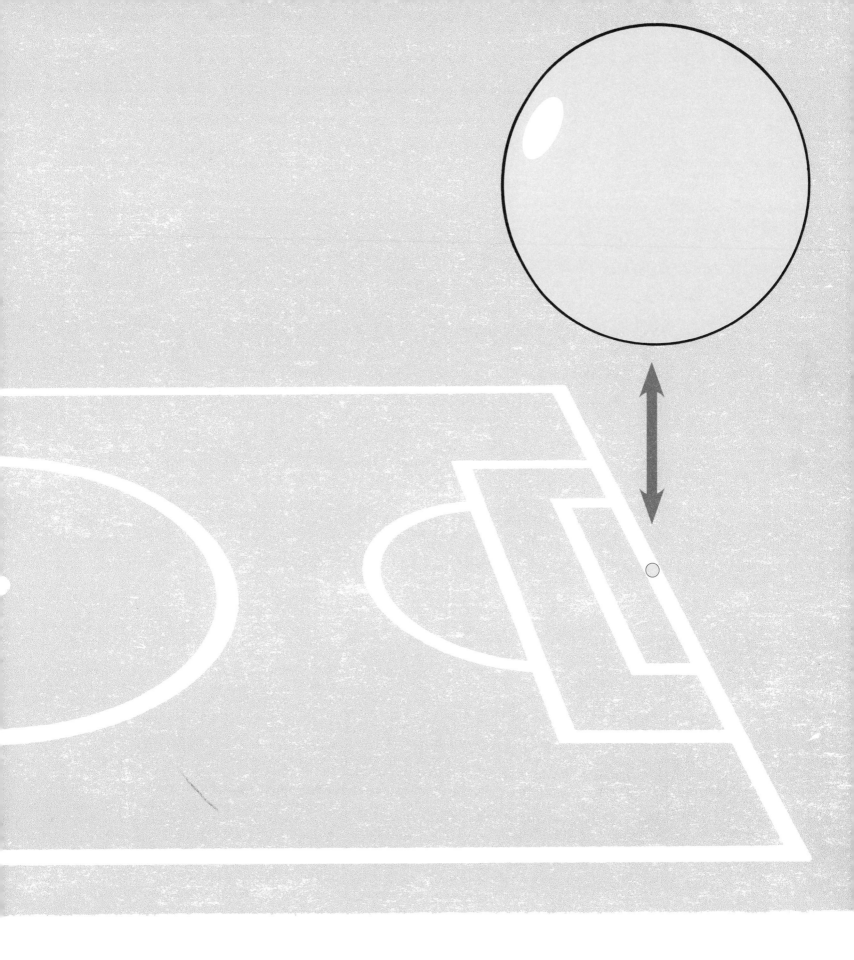

HOW FAST?

If you live fairly close to your school, you might be able to use your toy scooter to get there in about ten minutes. If it was on the moon, though, the ride would last 1,600 days, which is more than four years. Plus, the journey would take a lot longer if you actually stopped to rest and sleep. The sun is even farther away: you'd have to ride day and night for more than 1,700 years to get there. This is more than 600,000 days.

HOW FAR?

Snow leopards can out-jump any other animal in the world. The big cats can leap about 56 feet in one go, which means they could easily clear the length of a lorry truck! Let's compare that to the best we humans can do: the men's world record for the long jump is almost 30 feet, and the women's is nearly 25 feet. Those are pretty impressive distances, but they're still way too short to clear that bus.

56 feet

HOW FAST?

Imagine there's an elevator running right through the center of the Earth, connecting one side to the other. If you hopped aboard and traveled at an average elevator speed, the journey would last more than two weeks. Even if it was the fastest elevator in the world, you'd still be in there for eight days!

2 weeks

HOW FAST?

Cheetahs are brilliant short distance sprinters. They are capable of reaching a maximum running speed of around 68 miles per hour. Hence, these spotted predators are considered the fastest animals on the planet, on land that is! The sailfish can travel equally fast in water. Animals don't necessarily require four legs to be extremely fast. Sometimes two are just as good, for instance with the giant red kangaroo. It doesn't run, but jumps through Australia at almost 56 miles per hour. They reach a maximum speed of 55 miles per hour to be exact, which exceeds the maximum running speed of gazelles, wildebeests, and even lions.

56 miles per hour

68 miles per hour

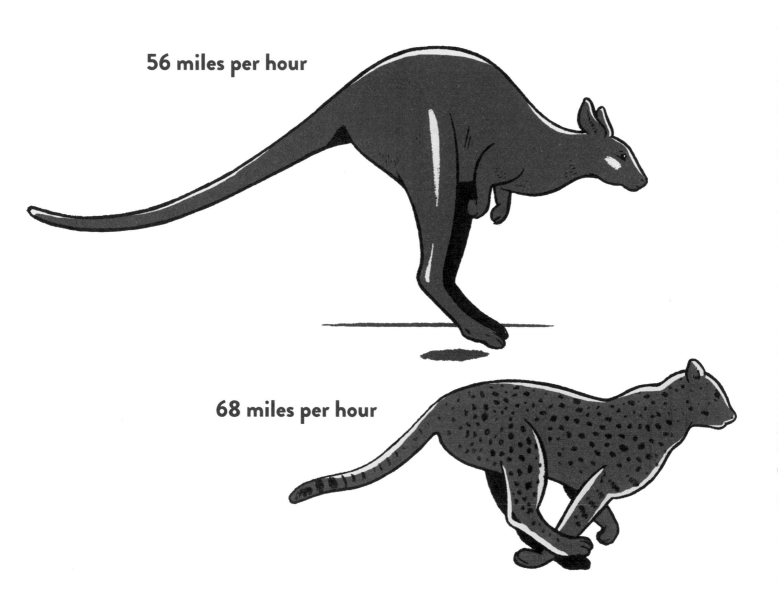

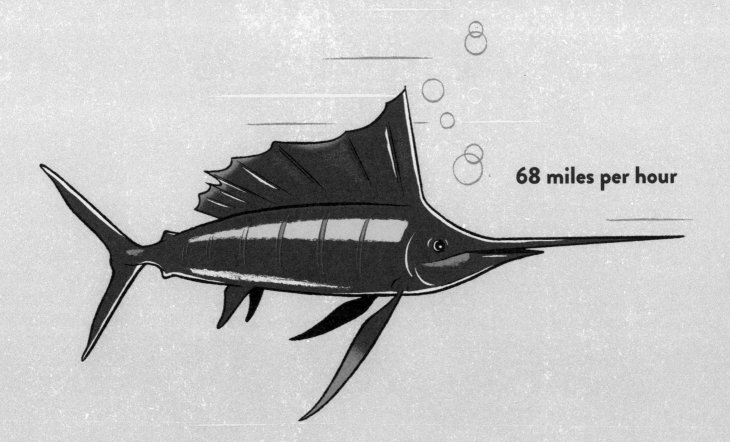

68 miles per hour

HOW SLOW?

When getting from A to B, birds are pretty fast. Many of them travel at 62 miles per hour. So does flying only work at high speeds? Not at all, the slowest long distance flyer is the sandpiper, with a maximum speed of 5 miles per hour. You can easily run at that speed, if not faster!

5 miles per hour

HOW MUCH?

A large male killer whale (orca) will grow to nearly 33 feet long and has to consume roughly 290,000 calories a day. If it only ate ice cream for instance, it would need to get through 1,500 scoops before bedtime. Alternatively, it could have 500 bars (110 pounds) of chocolate. Orcas aren't big fans of candy, though—they prefer to hunt fish. And since most fish only contain 150 to 200 calories per 3.5 ounces (chocolate contains 600 calories for the same weight), the whales have to eat roughly 320 to 430 pounds of fish a day!

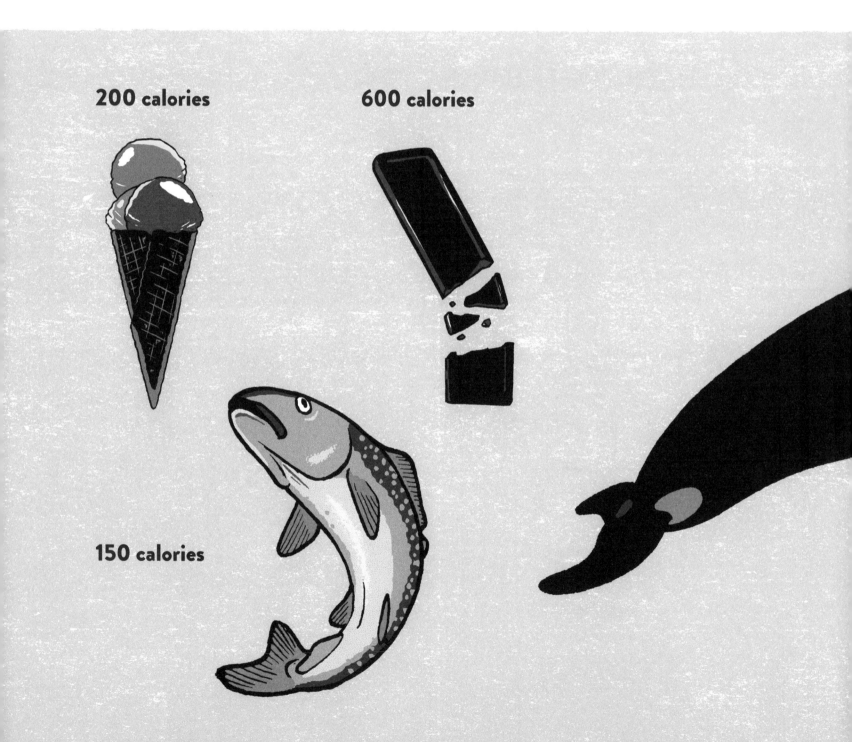

200 calories

600 calories

150 calories

HOW OLD?

Tortoises can live much longer than humans. When the world's oldest tortoise was born around the year 1825, there were no such things as electricity, telephones, cars, or airplanes!

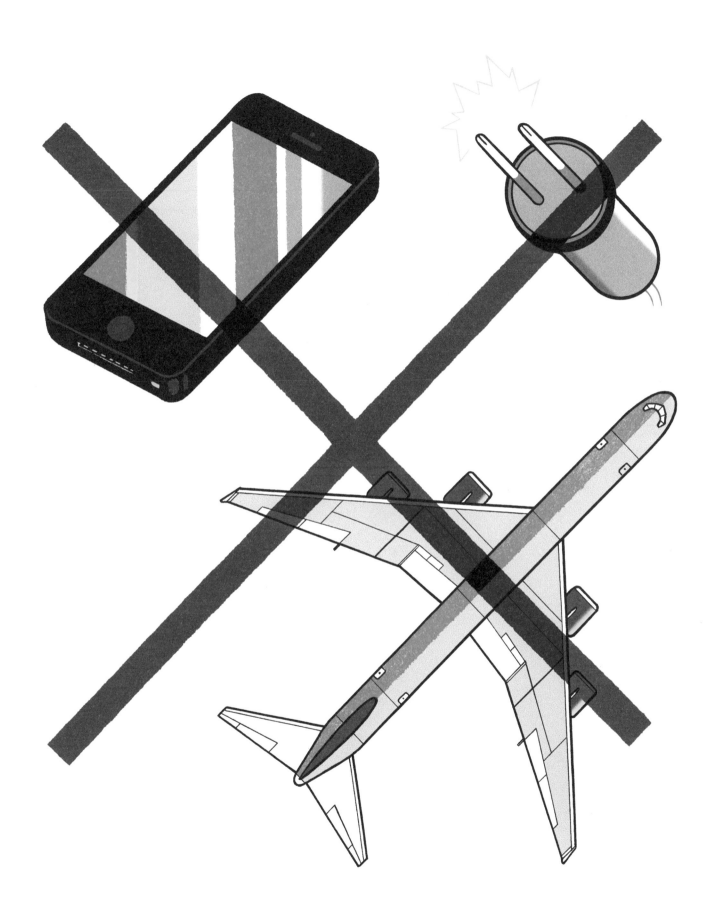

HOW OLD?

Longevity varies greatly depending on the species. Mosquitoes have a life expectancy of only a few weeks, so one day for a mosquito would be the equivalent of several years for humans. Likewise, a seven year old rabbit is already nearing the end of its life. Size has nothing to do with it—even some very big animals have shorter lifespans than ours, such as the humpback whale that usually only reaches 48 years of age. The Galápagos giant tortoise, on the other hand, can live to be 190 years old!

1 day

7 years

48 years

85 years **190 years**

HOW FAST?

When you call out to your friends, they hear you immediately. That's not surprising, as the speed of sound travels at 1,125 feet per second. That's the equivalent of 746 miles per hour. Nonetheless, at this speed, sound would still need 10 hours to travel around the globe once.

746 miles per hour

The speed of light is almost one million times faster than the speed of sound. It's hard to imagine, but light travels at a speed of 670,000 miles per hour. So at this speed it takes 0.13 seconds to go once around the globe. Also, light only needs 8.5 minutes to cover the distance from the sun to the Earth.

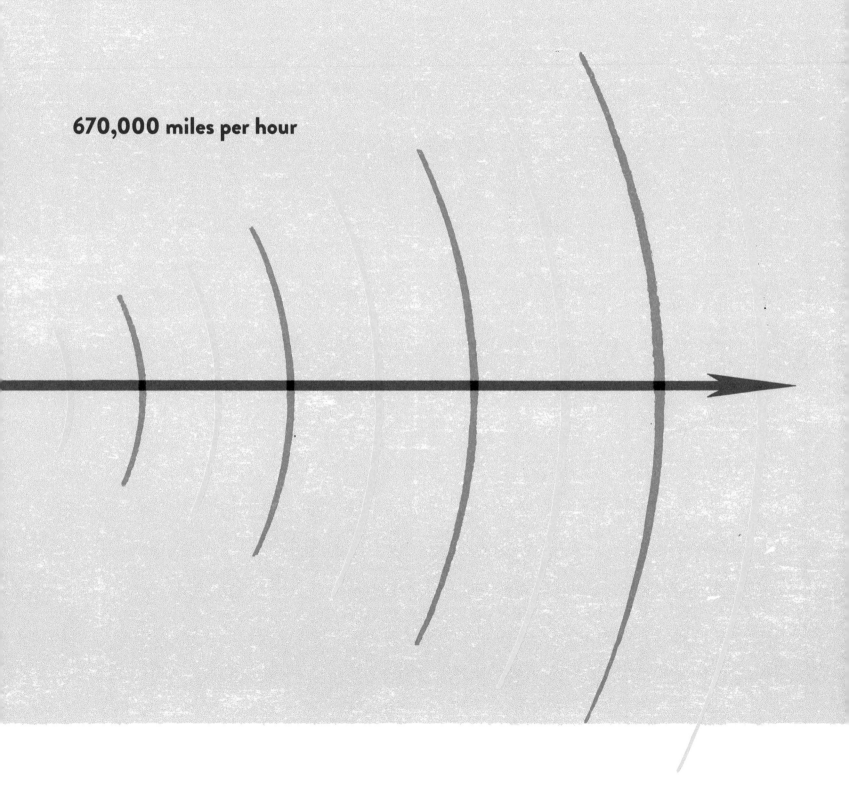

670,000 miles per hour

HOW BIG?

The Brookesia micra chameleon is the world's smallest known reptile. It grows to just an inch in length and can sit comfortably on a match. The Vervain hummingbird is another small wonder that is only about 2 inches in length, and builds a nest that is roughly half as big as a walnut shell. The record for the biggest eyes (among vertebrates that live on land) is held by the world's largest and heaviest bird: the ostrich. Its eyes are about 2 inches in diameter—that's roughly the width of your wrist.

1 inch

2 inches

HOW BIG?

Never get into a collision with a hippopotamus if you can help it. The heaviest hippos weigh nearly 10,000 pounds. That's the equivalent of having 50 big men stand on a scale at the same time. Weirdly, though, a hippo's brain is tiny. At 3.5 pounds, it is roughly the size of a human brain, which averages about 3 pounds.

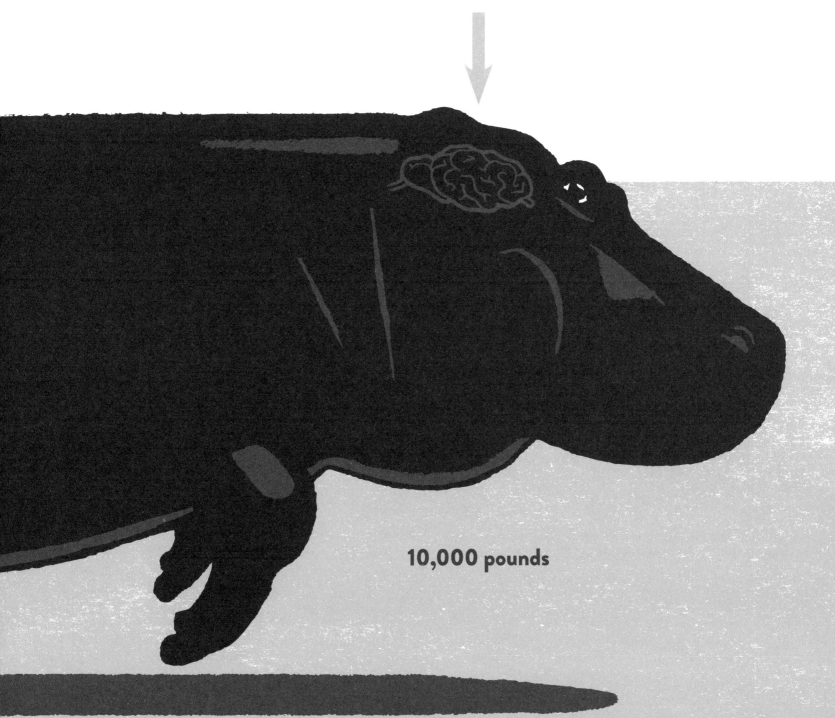

3.5 pounds

10,000 pounds

HOW MUCH?

The Komodo dragon is the biggest lizard in the world. It's not super heavy (it weighs 110 pounds on average) but boy, can it eat! A Komodo dragon can easily put away up to 80 percent of its bodyweight in one sitting. That's about 88 pounds of food. People in the United States eat roughly 3.2 pounds of food a day—from cereal at breakfast to ice cream after dinner—which is about 3 percent of their bodyweight.

110 pounds

165 pounds

HOW STRONG?

Size and muscles aren't everything. The world's strongest animal is the rhinoceros beetle. It's really small—about 1.5 inches long—but it can lift up to 850 times its own bodyweight. Ants are also pretty strong. They can carry 50 to 60 times their own weight. Humans lag way behind these mighty insects. For us, it's a struggle to lift even the equivalent of our own weight. If adults had the same strength as an ant, they would be able to carry a tractor weighing nearly 4.5 tons.

HOW BIG?

Some animals are bigger than you might think. A blue whale is so huge that its heart is the size of a small car and can weigh just as much (roughly 3,500 pounds). The blue whale also has the biggest tongue in the animal kingdom. It's ten feet thick and weighs about four tons, which makes it as heavy as an elephant! When a blue whale is swimming, you don't see its tongue because it rolls it up in its mouth.

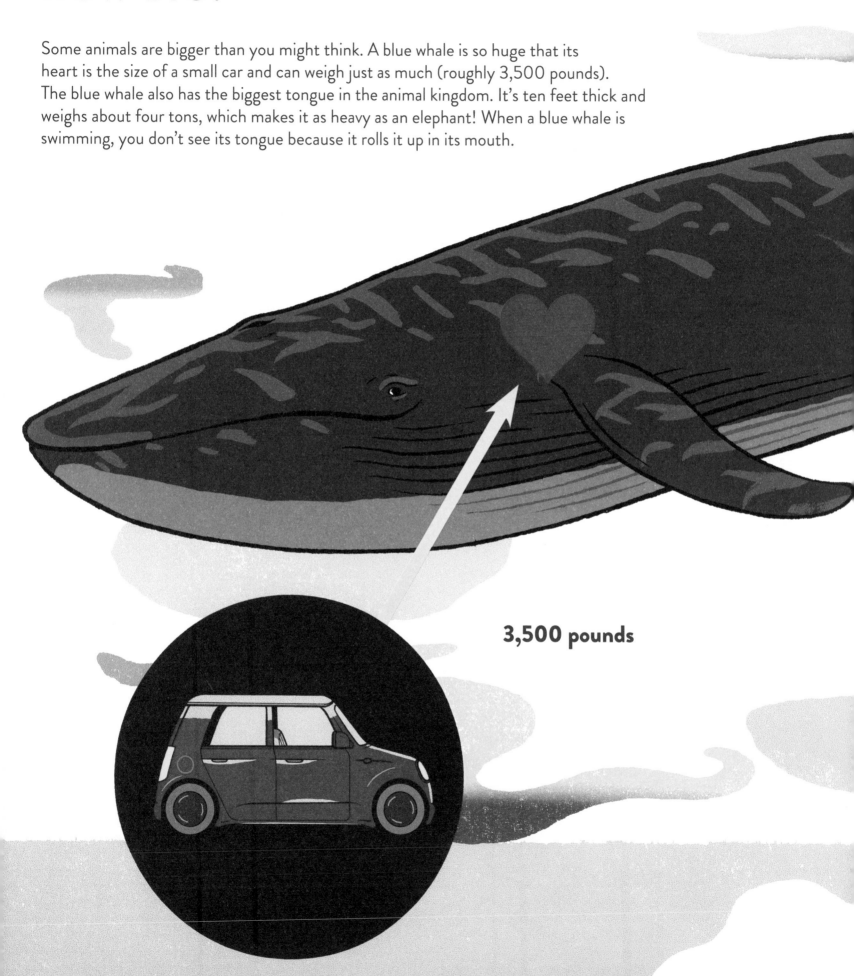

3,500 pounds

HOW BIG?

Elephants are the world's heaviest animals living on land, weighing an average of 10,000 pounds. It would take almost 60 fully-grown men weighing 180 pounds each to reach that weight! Cars weigh a little bit less at approximately 3,500 pounds, which would be more than 300 small poodles!

0.0001 pounds   **11 pounds**   **180 pounds**

3,500 pounds

10,000 pounds

HOW BIG IS BIG?
HOW FAR IS FAR?

by Jan van der Veken

Texts by Dorothee Soehlke-Lennert
Translation from German by Jen Metcalf
Editorial support by Kathrin Lilienthal

Published by Little Gestalten, Berlin 2015
ISBN 978-3-89955-732-9   (German Edition ISBN 978-3-89955-731-2)

Typeface: Brandon Grotesque by HVD Fonts
Printed by Livonia Print, Riga. Made in Europe

For more information, please visit www.little.gestalten.com.

Bibliographic information published by the Deutsche Nationalbibliothek.
The Deutsche Nationalbibliothek lists this publication in the Deutsche Nationalbibliografie; detailed bibliographic data are available online at http://dnb.d-nb.de.

This book was printed on paper certified according to the standards of the FSC®.

MIX
Paper from responsible sources
FSC® C002795
FSC
www.fsc.org